Working

by Joy Darlington

PEARSON

Scott
Foresman

Editorial Offices: Glenview, Illinois • Parsippany, New Jersey • New York, New York
Sales Offices: Needham, Massachusetts • Duluth, Georgia • Glenview, Illinois
Coppell, Texas • Sacramento, California • Mesa, Arizona

Learn about our **jobs**.

This is Joe.
He makes crayons.

This is Emma.
She takes care of children.

This is Maria.
She uses **tools** to fix things.

This is Oliver.
Oliver is a **volunteer**.
He works for free.

What job would you like to do? Why?

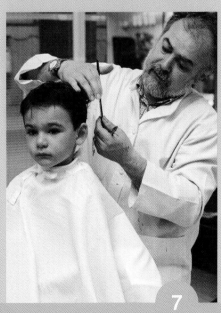

Glossary

job the work people do

tools things that are used to help people do work

volunteer a person who works for free

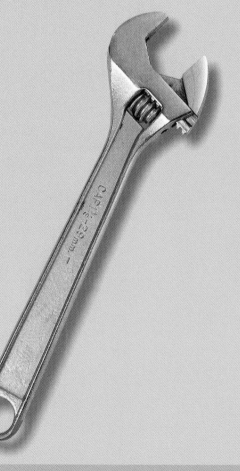